A Guide

The Courage of Sarah Noble

in the Classroom

Based on the book written by Alice Dalgliesh

This guide written by **Debra J. Housel**

Teacher Created Resources, Inc.
6421 Industry Way
Westminster, CA 92683
www.teachercreated.com

ISBN: 978-1-57690-642-2

©2000 Teacher Created Resources, Inc
Reprinted, 2008
Made in U.S.A.

Edited by
Lorin Klistoff, M.A.

Illustrated by
Sue Fullam

Cover Art by
Wendy Chang

Table of Contents

Introduction and Sample Lessons

A good book can touch the lives of children like a good friend. An interesting historical fiction book can teach children valuable information about a time period in our history, challenge their creativity, and inspire them to become better people. Therefore, great care has been taken in selecting the books and activities featured in the Literature Unit series. Although intended for use with primary students in grades one through three, some activities may require modification to meet the needs of students of varying ability levels. (Several options are included in Suggestions for Using the Unit Activities, pages 7–10.) Activities from all academic subjects make this a unit which teaches and reinforces skills across the curriculum. Students will simultaneously enjoy the story and gain knowledge and skills in all areas.

You can choose one of the following methods.

Sample Lesson Plan

The Sample Lesson Plan on page 4 provides you with a specific set of introductory lesson plan suggestions for *The Courage of Sarah Noble.* Each of the lessons takes about a day to complete if you do all of the suggested activities. Cover a chapter a day for 10 days, combining chapters 10 and 11 on the last day of the unit. Refer to Suggestions for Using the Unit Activities for information relating to the unit activities.

Unit Planner

If you wish to tailor the suggestions on pages 7–10 to a format other than the one prescribed, a blank Unit Planner is provided on page 5. On a specific day, you may choose activities you wish to include by writing the activity number or a brief notation about the lesson in the Unit Activities section. Space has also been provided for reminders, comments, and other pertinent information related to each day's activities. Reproduce copies of the Unit Planner as needed.

Sample Lesson Plan

Lesson 1
- Introduce the unit using any or all of the Before the Book activities on page 7.
- Read and discuss the preface with the children.
- Read About the Author on page 6.
- Introduce Chapter 1 vocabulary, page 16.
- Follow the suggestion for the phonics lesson for Chapter 1, page 18. Then read Chapter 1.

Lesson 2
- Introduce Chapter 2 vocabulary, page 16.
- Follow the suggestion for the phonics lesson for Chapter 2, page 18. Then read Chapter 2.
- Do the pocket chart activity to learn about wool processing techniques, page 13.
- Have children use a Connecticut map on page 33 to complete the activity on page 32.

Lesson 3
- Introduce Chapter 3 vocabulary, page 16.
- Follow the suggestion for the phonics lesson for Chapter 3, page 18. Then read Chapter 3.
- Ask the story questions for Chapters 1–3 on page 17.

Lesson 4
- Introduce Chapter 4 vocabulary, page 16.
- Follow the suggestion for the phonics lesson for Chapter 4, page 18. Then read Chapter 4.
- Do the math work sheet on general store supplies, page 29.
- Begin an animal research project, page 27.
- Have children do the coloring as you read the script for food processing techniques in the 1700s, pages 34–36.

Lesson 5
- Introduce Chapter 5 vocabulary, page 16.
- Follow the suggestion for the phonics lesson for Chapter 5, page 18. Then read Chapter 5.
- Continue the animal research project.
- Have the children make a Venn diagram, comparing themselves to Sarah, page 8.
- Have children design Sarah's quilt, pages 40 and 41.
- Do the Directed Manipulatives and Center Activities, page 31.

Lesson 6
- Introduce Chapter 6 vocabulary, page 16.
- Follow the suggestion for the phonics lesson for Chapter 6, page 18. Then read Chapter 6.
- Play some of the games Sarah played with the Indian children, pages 38 and 39.
- Continue working on the animal research project.
- Complete the cloze paragraph on page 28.
- Have the children choose one of the culminating projects and begin to create it, pages 44–46.

Lesson 7
- Introduce Chapter 7 vocabulary, page 16.
- Follow the suggestion for the phonics lesson for Chapter 7, page 18. Then read Chapter 7.
- Compose a biographical poem about Sarah Noble, page 19.
- Continue working on the animal research project.
- Continue the culminating project.

Lesson 8
- Introduce Chapter 8 vocabulary, page 16.
- Follow the suggestion for the phonics lesson for Chapter 8, page 18. Then read Chapter 8.
- Finish the animal research project.
- Do some more of the games Sarah played with the Indian children, pages 38 and 39.
- Have students color a page about wigwam construction, page 37.
- Continue the culminating project.

Lesson 9
- Introduce Chapter 9 vocabulary, page 16.
- Follow the suggestion for the phonics lesson for Chapter 9, page 18. Then read Chapter 9.
- Have students make tree booklets, pages 20–23.
- Do the math Word Problems on page 30.
- Have children play some physical education games based on Indian traditions, page 42.
- Continue the culminating project.

Lesson 10
- Introduce Chapters 10 and 11 vocabulary, page 16.
- Follow the suggestion for the phonics lesson for Chapters 10 and 11, page 18. Then read Chapters 10 and 11.
- Complete the log cabin sequencing of events on pages 25 and 26.
- Review story events with the crossword puzzle on page 24.
- Have children comment on the book via the Internet, page 43.
- Complete the culminating project.

4

Unit Planner

Unit Activities

Date: ⬭

Notes:

Unit Activities

Date: ⬭

Notes:

Unit Activities

Date: ⬭

Notes:

Unit Activities

Date: ⬭

Notes:

Unit Activities

Date: ⬭

Notes:

Unit Activities

Date: ⬭

Notes:

Getting to Know the Book and the Author

Book Summary

(Available in the USA from Aladdin Paperbacks, 1991; Canada, Distican; UK, Simon & Schuster; AUS, Prentice Hall)

The Courage of Sarah Noble details the true story of an 8-year-old girl who, at the turn of the eighteenth century, accompanied her father on a journey from Massachusetts to Connecticut. She served as his companion and cook while he built a log cabin on a homestead he had purchased from men in New Milford, Connecticut. Theirs was the first house erected in New Milford, Connecticut. When her father completed the home, he left Sarah with a Native American family with whom they had developed a friendship while he returned to Westfield, Massachusetts, to retrieve the rest of their large family.

Throughout the initial journey, during the months spent living in a cave while their home was being erected and during the time spent living with the Native Americans, Sarah felt genuinely afraid and had her courage tested many times. By repeating her mother's inspirational words, "Keep up your courage, Sarah Noble," the child managed to triumph over her fear and eventually be joyously reunited with her mother and siblings.

About the Author

Alice Dalgliesh was born on October 7, 1893, in Trinidad, British West Indies, and while a child, she became a naturalized American citizen when her parents moved to the United States. She spent her early childhood years in an isolated island setting, which resulted in her repeatedly rereading all the books her family owned. She attributed her lifelong love of books and reading to this early immersion in literature.

Dalgliesh earned a degree in elementary education and served as a primary teacher for 17 years before working as a children's book editor for Charles Scribner's Sons in New York City from 1934 to 1960. Her keen understanding of what made ideal material for children led to her appointment as the first president of the Children's Book Council.

Dalgliesh's writings establish her as a pioneer in the field of children's historical fiction. She detested almost all informational books directed at children and felt they "turned children off" to reading nonfiction. Instead, she said, "Facts must be cloaked in a fictional context. Children must become involved in a story that has bits of information tucked in deftly here and there." All 40 of her books, including her three Newbery Honor books, *The Silver Pencil, The Courage of Sarah Noble,* and *Bears on Hemlock Mountain,* reflect this attitude.

Throughout her years in New York City, she spent as much time as possible during the summers in Woodbury, Connecticut, just a few miles from the site of Sarah Noble's original house. In fact, Dalgliesh's house was built less than 10 years after Sarah's. This fact was Dalgliesh's original motivation to discover more about the history of the area. She retired to this house and lived there until her death on June 11, 1979.

(References for this biographical sketch are from *Something About the Author*, Volume 17, pages 47–52.)

6

Suggestions for Using the Unit Activities

Use some or all of the following suggestions to introduce your students to *The Courage of Sarah Noble* and to extend their appreciation of the book through activities that cross the curriculum. The suggested activities have been divided into three sections to assist you in planning the literature unit. These sections are as follows:

- Before the Book includes suggestions for preparing the classroom environment and the students for the literature to be read.
- Into the Book has activities that focus on the book's content, characters, theme, etc.
- After the Book extends the readers' enjoyment of the book and solidifies knowledge gained during the unit through two culminating activities.

Before the Book

1. Introduce the unit by reading the book's preface and discussing it with the children.

2. Read About the Author on page 6, and explain how Alice Dalgliesh was a pioneer in historical fiction for children.

3. To activate background knowledge and oral language skills, ask the children what they know about Indians and the settlers in New England.

4. Share whatever information you feel is appropriate from Notes on Indians in Connecticut, circa 1707 on page 11.

5. Show students where Massachusetts and Connecticut are on a United States map.

6. To increase interest in the story, ask students to write a paragraph about a time when they were frightened or separated from their home and parent. If they are very young, students may volunteer to talk about such an event.

7. Introduce the vocabulary for each chapter to the students by doing any of the following:

   - Print the words on chart paper, an overhead transparency, or the board.
   - Ask volunteers to define the words.
   - Use the pocket chart cards.
   - Once a word has been defined, ask the children to write a sentence using the word in their classroom journal.

8. Introduce the phonics focus for each chapter (page 18) to the students by doing any of the following:

   - Discuss common word parts and how their recognition helps increase decoding skills.
   - Use the words as spelling words, emphasizing their common word parts.
   - Put up a word wall about common word parts.
   - Have a "treasure hunt." Tell the children the word part of the day and then have them write down an example each time they encounter it as they read that chapter. (**Note:** Tell them how many there are to find in advance.)
   - Use the words as flash cards to reinforce specific word parts.

Suggestions for Using the Unit Activities *(cont.)*

Into the Book

1. Pocket Chart

- Make copies of the wigwam (pattern on page 14) and put a vocabulary word from the list on page 16 on each wigwam. Use the "wigwam words" to introduce and reinforce vocabulary.

- Make copies of Sarah's cloak (pattern on page 14) and write a story question from page 17 on each one. Use the "cloak questions" to lead class discussion at the end of every three chapters to develop critical thinking skills and promote comprehension.

- To do a guided discovery lesson on how wool gets from a sheep into a cloak, cut out and laminate the wool processing pictures on page 15, and then follow the directions given on page 13. This is an excellent way to develop logical reasoning, sequencing skills, and oral-language skills.

2. Language Arts

- There are at least 30 words that can be made with the letters in the word COURAGE. Challenge the students to find as many words as they can. Explain that each letter can be used only once.

- Develop sequencing skills by copying the sentence strips and the log cabin on pages 25 and 26. Have the children glue the events on the logs to the side of the cabin in the order in which they occurred in the story.

- Review vocabulary. Ask them to choose five of them and write a sentence using each. The sentences must be about *The Courage of Sarah Noble.*

- Enhance character identification by having the children complete a Venn diagram comparing themselves to Sarah.

- Have students write and illustrate the Biographical Poem about Sarah on page 19. This will be easier if they have done a Venn diagram beforehand.

- Make little books on the trees in the Connecticut wilderness by copying pages 20–23 for each student. Have the children construct the tree booklets by cutting out the leaves, gluing them on the corresponding pages, and assembling the booklet. Ask them to practice reading it to you, friends, and parents.

- Teach a lesson on how to format and write personal letters. On the board or an overhead projector, write a letter telling Sarah Noble about a time when you showed courage. On the first three lines in the upper right-hand corner, write your return address followed by the date. (**Note:** Do not include your name here.) On the set of lines at the left, put *Miss Sarah Noble, New Milford, CT* (called inside address). For the salutation use *Dear Sarah* followed by a comma, and for the closing start at the center, use *Sincerely yours* or *Yours truly* followed by a comma. Beneath the closing, sign your name. Have the children compose and edit their letters on scrap paper prior to completing a final copy. Once the student letters are done, choose some volunteers to share theirs with the class or post all the letters on a bulletin board or wall.

Suggestions for Using the Unit Activities *(cont.)*

Into the Book *(cont.)*

2. Language Arts *(cont.)*

- When the students have completed the crossword puzzle on page 24, they will have reviewed the entire book. To make the puzzle more challenging or to use it as a quiz, cover the list of words prior to photocopying the page.

3. Science

- Almost every animal mentioned in the book is warm blooded (the one exception is fish). Review the details about the two kinds of warm-blooded animals (birds and mammals).

- Teach the use of reference materials by asking each child to research an animal mentioned in the book, page 27. They can use traditional and/or electronic reference materials.

- Do a mini lesson in botany by having the children complete the cloze paragraph on strawberries, page 28.

4. Math

- Have the children calculate the cost of the supplies that John Noble bought at the general store by completing page 29. For children for whom this math is too advanced, make it into a group lesson on how to use a calculator. (**Note:** If using metrics, convert measurements accordingly before reproducing the page.)

- Sharpen your children's ability to do word problems with page 30. For children for whom this math is too advanced, make it into a group lesson on mathematical reasoning. Choose a few of the problems to pose to the class, asking, "How would we go about solving this problem? What information do we have? What information do we need? Can we make a picture to help us solve it? Is there another way to solve it? Could we use manipulatives (e.g., chips, craft sticks) and count up to the answer?" (**Note:** If using metrics, convert measurements accordingly before reproducing the page.)

- Develop your students' geometric knowledge with Directed Manipulatives and Center Activities on page 31.

5. Social Studies

- Help your students exercise reasoning skills to discover how wool gets from a sheep and into Sarah's cloak by doing the pocket chart activity outlined on page 13.

- Help your students interpret the map of Western Connecticut on pages 32 and 33.

- Teach the students a lesson in how difficult it was to keep food from spoiling by talking them through the food-drying process. Use the script and coloring page found on pages 34–36.

- Teach your class one or all of the traditional Indian games on pages 38 and 39 to help them experience the Indian culture in the same way that Sarah did when she played with the Indian children.

- Enhance students' understanding of how Sarah lived with Tall John and his family in the wigwam by having the children color page 37.

Suggestions for Using the Unit Activities *(cont.)*

Into the Book *(cont.)*

6. Art

- Give students a chance to express themselves by designing Sarah's quilt using the pattern pieces on page 40 and the quilt block on page 41. This activity promotes important visualization skills. Whenever Sarah's quilt is mentioned in the book, stop and ask the students to close their eyes and "make a photograph" in their minds of the scene. When the children have completed their quilt blocks, glue them all together on a large piece of butcher paper and display the class quilt in the classroom or hallway under a banner titled "Sarah Noble's Quilt, circa 1707."

7. Physical Education

- Several active games are given on page 42 that you or the gym teacher can teach your class to help them experience the Indian culture in the same way that Sarah did when she played with the Indian children. Prior to having the children play these games, explain the reasons why Indian children played these games (listed at the top of page 42).

8. Technology

- Have the children reflect on their feelings about *The Courage of Sarah Noble*. Write the sentence starters given on page 43 on the board or overhead or photocopy them and have students complete the sentences. Ask them to choose one of their sentences to include as they act as reviewers of the book at the amazon.com Web site. Plan to visit the site a month or so after this activity to show the children that their opinions remain there for anyone in the world to read.

After the Book

Two culminating activities are thoroughly explained on pages 44–46. If viable in your classroom, you can choose to make both an available option, and then let the students decide which one they would prefer to do:

1. Stick Puppet Theater

For this, you will need to help make a theater, following the suggestions given on page 44. You can reproduce the stick puppet figures on page 45 and have the children assemble and decorate them. Assign small groups of three to five children to write a script outlining the most important events in the story. For greater challenge, have the students create a new adventure for Sarah Noble, using the puppets and theater to tell their stories. If additional characters are needed, the students can make their own puppets. Each small group of students can take turns reading the parts and using the stick puppets while the rest of the class serves as an audience. These skits can also be performed for another teacher's class, school administrators, or parents. This project is motivational for tactile/kinesthetic learners who may not enjoy writing assignments. With the anticipation of acting it out, they may actually enjoy writing the scripts.

2. 18th Century Dioramas

This is also a good way for tactile learners to solidify understanding in an enjoyable way and may be a better choice for younger students as it requires no writing. Have the children create an 18th century diorama by organizing the children into groups of three and requesting that each group build a model of Tall John's wigwam or the Nobles' log cabin. More extensive suggestions are given on page 46.

     10

Notes on Indians in Connecticut, circa 1707

Very sparse definitive information exists regarding the Indians in Connecticut at the time Sarah Noble arrived on the banks of the Housatonic River. The approximately 100 tribes were extremely small—often no bigger than an extended family—and had loose associations with one another. Rather than stand up to the invaders to protect their land, the tiny tribes had great infighting, and it was a sorrowfully simple matter for the whites to stir up animosity amongst them and get them to kill off each other. Since European diseases had wiped out 75 percent of the native population with the arrival of the whites during the 17th century, only remnants of the original Indian population remained by 1707, and these moved about frequently as no real territorial boundaries seemed to exist.

Based on research, it is probable that the Paugusset were the Indians who befriended the Nobles, as they seem to have been located on the eastern side of the Housatonic River near New Milford. However, information about this tiny tribe is negligible, so throughout the book information is given about the Algonquin Indians, of whom all Eastern Woodlands Indians are considered a part. Also included are games from the Mahicans, one of the more cohesive and larger Connecticut tribes occupying the region from what is now the New York state border to the western bank of the Housatonic River. Although the Connecticut Indians seemed to be continually at war with one another, their cultures appear to have been identical, and whatever caused the conflicts prior to the settlers' arrival is unknown. Therefore, the following is basic information about Tall John and his tribe.

Food

Women tended small crops of corn, squash, and beans. They also ate and introduced the British to popcorn, maple sugar, and wild rice. For meat, they ate deer and any small animals they could capture with a bow and arrow (raccoon, woodchuck, turkey, etc.).

Shelter

Each family had its own wigwam. There were about 10 to 50 wigwams in a village, often surrounded by a stockade. Wigwams were oval frames of poles built in a dome shape and covered with slabs of elm bark, birch bark, or woven cattail stalks. In winter, all three would be used as coverings to insulate the dwelling. The floor was hard-packed earth with a fire in the center for cooking and to give warmth. A smoke hole directly above the fire could be vented by means of an outdoor pole with a piece of deerskin lashed to it. This was moved about to ensure that no smoke was trapped in the wigwam. Around the inside of the structure, platforms provided seats and beds.

Clothing

Much to the dismay of the Europeans, Indian children went naked during the summer until they reached the age of 9 or 10. After that and during the colder months, males wore moccasins, leggings, a breechcloth, and a robe, all made of deerskin. Females wore moccasins, leggings, and a skirt formed by folding a rectangular piece at the waist, all made of deerskin. Clothing the upper part of the body was optional for both males and females.

Government

The basic Indian government, called a council, held a powwow whenever the elders felt an important discussion was necessary. At these meetings, the adult Indians—male and female—gathered around a large fire to talk about problems, generate solutions, and make decisions. As part of this process, they said prayers, danced, and sang songs, usually accompanied by drums and rattles. The Iroquois were powerful enemies that lay across the Hudson River.

Other

They had not learned to weave cloth but were skillful at making woven bags, mats, and baskets. They moved around a great deal and often had a summer camp that was different from their winter one.

Pocket Chart Activities

Prepare a pocket chart for sorting and using vocabulary cards, story question cards, and sentence strips. Use a commercial pocket chart, or if necessary, you can make a pocket chart if you have access to a laminator.

How to Make a Pocket Chart

Begin by laminating a 24" x 36" (61 cm x 91 cm) piece of heavyweight colored tagboard. To make nine pockets, cut a sheet of clear plastic into nine 2" x 20" (5 cm x 50 cm) strips. Equally space the strips down the 36" (91 cm) length of the tagboard. Attach each strip with clear packing tape along the sides and bottom. This will hold the sentence strips, word cards, etc., and can be displayed in a learning center or mounted on a chalk tray or easel for use with a group.

How to Use the Pocket Chart

1. Reproduce the wigwam pattern on page 14 onto oaktag or other heavy paper. Make vocabulary cards from the lists given on page 16. Place them on the pocket chart one at a time as you present the vocabulary prior to each chapter or when you discuss the word parts in the spelling words.

2. Some time after introducing the words (perhaps as review after reading a chapter or two), put the vocabulary cards up on the chart and play Word Sleuth with the children. Tell them that you are thinking of one of the words on the pocket chart and give them clues to guess it; the students get to make a guess after each clue is given.

    Example: Clue 1: "I'm thinking of a word with six letters." *(Students take a guess.)*

    Clue 2: "It has two vowels." *(Students take a guess.)*

    Clue 3: "It means serious." *(Students will probably guess the word "solemn" within three clues.)*

3. Reproduce copies of the cloak pattern on page 14 on six different colors of construction paper or oaktag. Use a different color of paper for each level of Bloom's taxonomy. Write the story questions from page 17 on the appropriate color-coded cloak. Write the level of the question on the back of the card. Laminate the cloaks for durability.

Example:

    I. Knowledge *(pink)*

    II. Comprehension *(yellow)*

    III. Application *(green)*

    IV. Analysis *(blue)*

    V. Synthesis *(lavender)*

    VI. Evaluation *(orange)*

Who is the book's main character?

Pocket Chart Activities *(cont.)*

How to Use the Pocket Chart *(cont.)*

3. *(cont.)*

After reading *The Courage of Sarah Noble,* provide opportunities for the children to develop and practice higher-level critical-thinking skills by using the color-coded cloaks in some or all of the following ways:

- Use a specific color-coded set of cards to question students at a particular level of learning.
- Have a child choose a card and read it aloud or give it to the teacher to read aloud. The child answers the question or calls on a volunteer to answer it.
- Pair the children. The teacher reads a question. The partners take turns responding to the question.

4. Use sentence strips to practice oral reading and sequencing of the story events. If possible, laminate them for durability.

5. Guide the discovery of the process of making wool cloth. Reproduce the picture cards on page 15 and place them on the chart in random order. Seat the children in a circle around the pocket chart. Tell them that the 10 cards on the chart are the 10 steps in the process used to get wool from a sheep's body and into the red cloak Sarah wore. Without discussing the process in advance, ask the children to make logical predictions as to which step is first. Once a volunteer has offered the first step, consult the rest of the group to see if they agree that it should be the first step. Follow the same procedure for the second and subsequent steps. Do not give the children hints nor tell them if they are right or wrong; merely ask leading questions, such as . . .

- "Does that make sense?"
- "Would that be the next step?"
- "Should any other picture up here come before this?"
- "What should be next?" and "Why do you think so?"
- "Do you agree?"

Even when the children make errors, do not stop them. They will eventually discover it as they unravel the process step by step. This is an excellent opportunity to develop sequential, logical, and critical-thinking skills. When they finally have the entire process in the right order on the pocket chart, tape the cards in the correct order on a sheet of butcher paper for display in the classroom. You can also have the students describe the 10 steps to you as you write them on a sheet of butcher paper. Then they can copy the steps from the butcher paper into their journals as a handwriting exercise.

The 10 steps in their correct order are as follows:

1. sheep being sheared
2. wool being handwashed
3. wool being carded
4. wool going from card to spindle on spinning wheel
5. spinning wheel making thread

6. handloom weaving thread
7. fabric being dyed
8. scissors cutting the fabric
9. handsewing cloak together with needle and thread
10. Sarah wearing the cloak

Pocket Chart Patterns

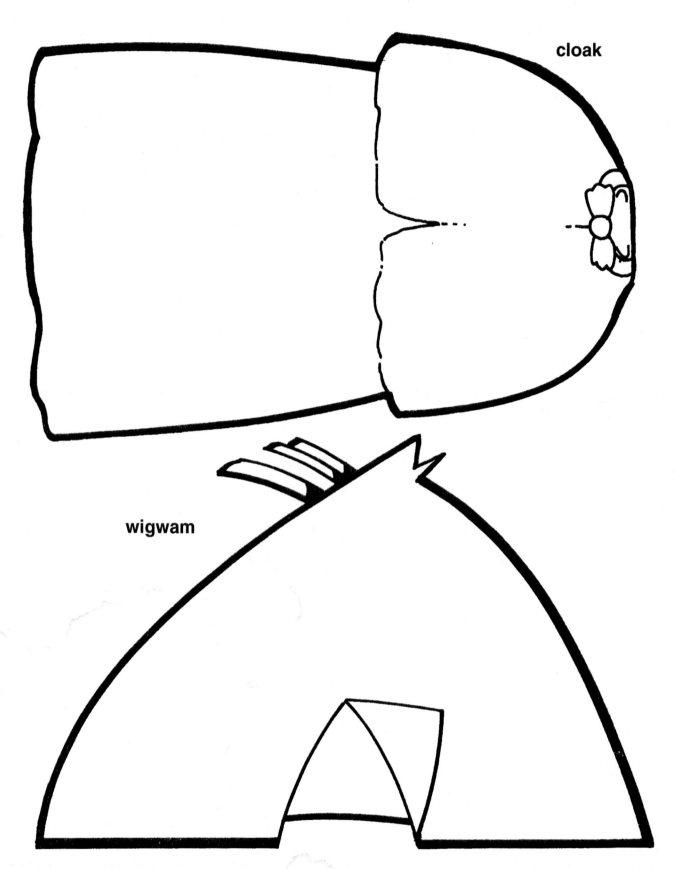

cloak

wigwam

Wool Processing Pictures

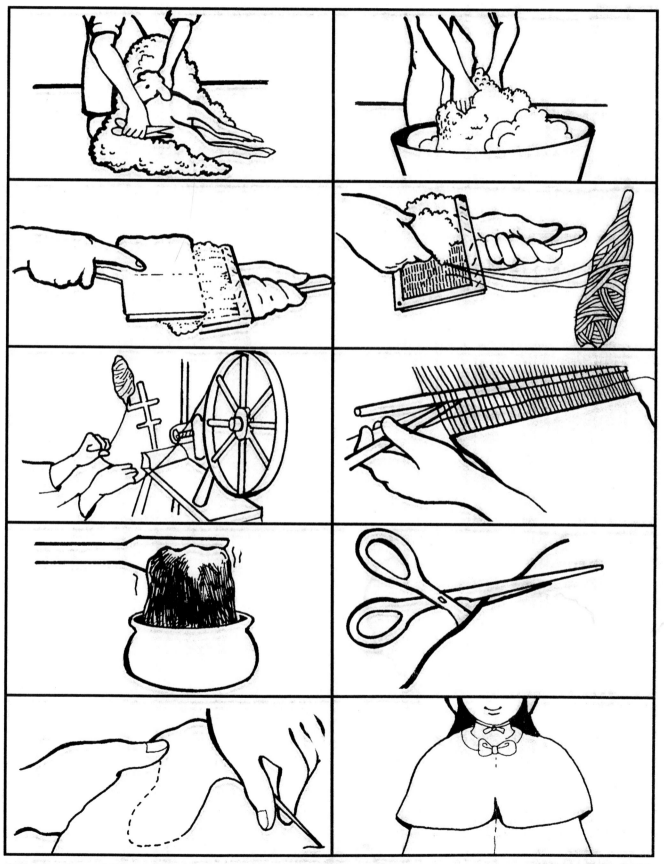

Vocabulary Word Lists

Introduce these vocabulary words prior to reading each chapter to ensure that the children have a basic understanding of their meanings.

Chapter 1	**Chapter 2**	**Chapter 3**
journey	settlement	harness
quilt	latch	hut
cloak	Massachusettes	solemn
courage	heathen	coarse
Connecticut	savages	misty
musket	timidly	wearily
fussing		

Chapter 4	**Chapter 5**	**Chapter 6**
Milford	steadily	serious
coast	namesake	mortar
johnnycake	rustling	pestle
porridge	clink	saddle bags
wove	palisade	
plots	petticoats	
woodchuck	impatience	

Chapter 7	**Chapter 8**	**Chapter 9**
scarlet	cornsilk	moccasins
squaw	choked	disturbance
mush	Great Spirit	scarcely
strides	wasting	sleep-breathing
mounting		crinkled
		tiresome
		dew

Chapter 10	**Chapter 11**
quivers	cozy
unsteady	wigwams
knelt	housekeeper
outlandish	height

Story Questions

To cover all of the levels of Bloom's taxonomy and promote higher-level thinking skills, ask the children all the questions in the column for each set of chapters. Be sure to ask the questions in the order given.

	Chapters 1 through 3	**Chapters 4 through 7**	**Chapters 8 through 11**
Knowledge	• Who is the book's main character? • With whom is she travelling?	• Where do Sarah and her father stay while the house is being built? • What book did Sarah read aloud to the Native American children?	• What did Sarah do before going to bed at night? • Who brings Sarah home to greet her mother, brothers, and sisters?
Comprehension	• Where are Sarah and her father travelling? • Why are they going there?	• What things frighten Sarah? • What happened when the Native American children first approached Sarah?	• Does Sarah like Tall John's wife's cooking? How do you know? • For whom does Sarah pray?
Application	• What does Sarah think when she first sees the valley where their house will be built? • Would you willingly go on Sarah's journey?	• What things did John Noble do to make the cave comfortable? • What possessions would you want to have with you in the cave if you were Sarah?	• Why did the first night with Tall John and his family seem strange to Sarah? • What is the difference between the way Sarah is used to eating and the way the Native Americans eat?
Analysis	• Why did Mrs. Noble tell Sarah to keep up her courage? • What might scare Sarah?	• Why did Sarah hold back her tears until her father had left? • What makes communicating with the Native Americans somewhat difficult?	• Why do you think Mrs. Noble doesn't believe the squaw could be as good a housekeeper or mother as she is? • What do you think might have happened if the watchers on Guarding Hill had sent a warning?
Synthesis	• Why does Sarah's father worry about bringing her along? • Why do you think Sarah asked her father not to shoot the deer?	• What might have happened if Sarah had refused to stay with Tall John's family? • Why was Sarah's father worried about leaving her with the Native Americans?	• How would Sarah have felt if her mother hadn't brought her doll, Arabella? • What do you think will happen next for the Noble family?
Evaluation	• Do you think the Robinsons could have been more welcoming? How? • Do you think the Native Americans will be friendly to Sarah and her father? Why?	• Could Sarah's first meeting with the Native American children have been more successful? How? • Do you think there will be an attack from the northern Native American tribes? Why?	• What is the best part of the story? Why? • Why is it important that Sarah's courage always ... her?

Phonics

A crucial skill necessary for quick and effective decoding of words is the recognition of common word parts. The words listed below are in the order in which they appear in the chapter. The common word part on which to focus for each chapter is given in parentheses.

Chapter 1 *(igh)*	**Chapter 2** *(–ed)*		**Chapter 3** *(–ly)*		**Chapter 4** *(–er)*
night	seemed	stroked	suddenly	surely	river
goodnight	looked	smacked	terribly	carefully	father
light	knocked	added	lonely	only	larger
tightly	lifted	promised	friendly	firmly	weather
bright	seated	changed	fearfully	tightly	later
sighed	smiled	whispered	wearily		under
	laughed				mother
					her

Chapter 5 *(en)*		**Chapters 6 and 7** *(compounds)*	**Chapter 8** *(two sounds of oo)**	**Chapter 9** *(–ing)*	
fence	suddenly	sometimes	too	nothing	everything
spoken	then	strawberries	food	guarding	forgetting
entrance	when	cannot	soon	coming	charming
opened	often	woodpile	understood	calling	watching
listen	children	outside	good	wailing	saying
even	broken	breakfast	cooked	breathing	
		himself	looked		
		anything			

Chapters 10 *(e at the end makes the first vowel long)*	**Chapter 11** *(ee)*
home	asleep
fine	indeed
waded	see
beside	queer
raced	housekeeper
came	sleep
taken	trees
close	
those	

*Have children list words containing *oo* as they find them while reading this chapter. Then have them sort the words into the two sounds *oo* makes. Discuss which sound is the more common and, therefore, the first one to try when encountering an unknown word.

Biographical Poem

Directions: Think about the story. Then fill in the blanks below with your own words.

1. Sarah

2. _____, _____, _____, and _____
          (four character traits of Sarah)

3. _____ of _____
          (daughter of, friend of, sister of)

4. Who loves _____, _____, _____, and _____
          (four things or people)

5. Who feels _____, _____, _____, and _____

6. Who needs _____, _____, _____, and _____

7. Who fears _____, _____, _____, and _____

8. Who gives _____, _____, _____, and _____

9. Who would like to see _____, _____, and _____

10. Resident of _____

11. Noble

Now copy the biographical poem you have written onto a clean sheet of paper, *leaving out the words in parentheses and the line numbers.* Glue your final copy onto construction paper, and illustrate the border with clip art from the computer or with hand drawings.

Ideas for Illustrations

- Tall John
- Tall John's wigwam
- Sarah wearing her red cloak
- Sarah's quilt
- the log cabin John Noble built
- John Noble

- Thomas, the horse
- the Great River
- Sarah's doll, Arabella
- the cave
- Tall John's family
- Sarah dressed in Indian clothing

Making a Tree Book

Directions: Follow the steps below to make a tree book.

1. Cut out the pages of the book on pages 21–23.
2. Color the leaves and seed pictures below.
3. Cut out each picture and then glue it onto the correct pages of your book.
4. Put the pages of your book in order.
5. Staple your book along the top.
6. Read your book to your teacher, friends, and parents.

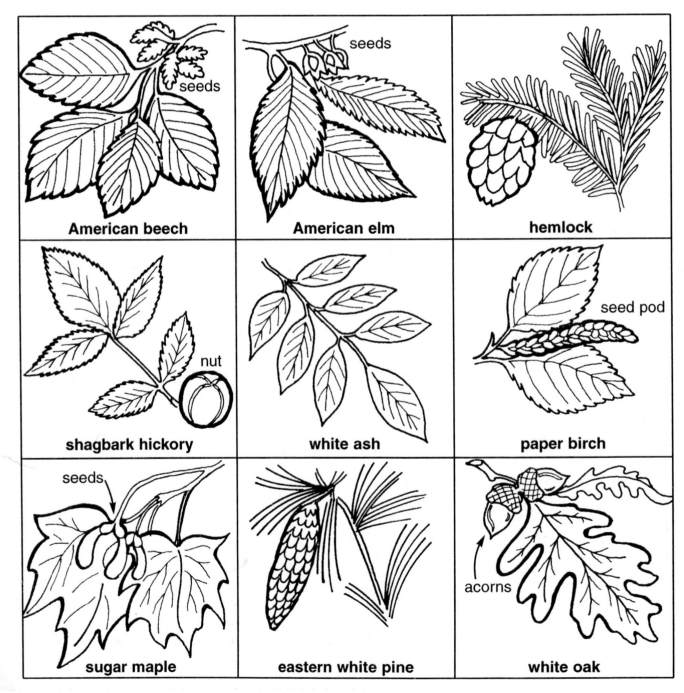

American beech	**American elm**	**hemlock**
shagbark hickory	**white ash**	**paper birch**
sugar maple	**eastern white pine**	**white oak**

Making a Tree Book (cont.)

My Book
of
Trees

by _____

Trees were very important to the Noble family. They used the wood from the trees for fuel and to make many things.

The trees in this book are the ones found in the forest around the Nobles' new home in Connecticut.

1

The Nobles used eastern white pine for logs to build their home, pitch to waterproof their roofs, and pine cones for fuel.

2

John Noble made the fence from American elm wood. Elm was also used to make small things such as boxes and buckets.

3

Making a Tree Book *(cont.)*

The bark of the American beech gave the Noble family writing paper and fuel.

4

Paper birch grew all along the Great River. Tall John's tribe used it to make canoes.

5

Burning shagbark hickory was used to smoke ham. This made it safe to eat for a long time. Hickory trees provided tasty nuts and could be used to make wagon wheels.

6

Each March, sugar maples delighted the Nobles by giving sap that they made into syrup and sugar.

7

Making a Tree Book *(cont.)*

The Nobles used white ash trees to make axe, hoe, rake, and hammer handles.

8

When boiled, hemlock's bark gives tannin. The Nobles needed tannin to change animal skins into leather.

9

Connecticut's state tree, white oak, had many uses, including making furniture, barrels, and boats. Wooden nails and table tops also came from these trees. Tall John's tribe ate its acorns during the long winters.

10

The End

11

Courageous Crossword Puzzle

Directions: Choose the right word from the list below to complete each clue, and fill it in on the puzzle. (Not all words will be used.)

Across

1. To keep warm, Sarah wore her _____.
2. While her father built the log cabin, he and Sarah lived in a _____.
3. Sarah's father built their new home in the _____.
4. John Noble used his _____ to shoot animals for them to eat.
5. Sarah's mother called the Indians _____.
6. For dinner, Sarah cooked bean _____.

Down

1. Sarah's mother told Sarah to keep up her _____.
3. Sarah stayed with Tall John's family in their _____.
6. Sarah worried that she was not _____ the first time she met the Indian children.
7. In the forest, Sarah slept on the ground by lying on her _____.
8. While she lived with the Indians, Sarah dressed in _____ made of deerskin.
9. Tall John's squaw made Sarah a beautiful pair of _____.

Answer Box				
wigwam	quilt	savages	wilderness	clothes
polite	porridge	cloak	moccasins	musket
brave	pebbles	cave	courage	palisade

Log Cabin Sequencing

Directions: Cut out each sentence strip. Arrange strips in the order of the events in the story. Number the strips 1–15. Glue strips 1–5 to the first log cabin (Chapters 1–3), strips 6–10 to the second log cabin (Chapters 4–7), and strips 11–15 to the third log cabin (Chapters 8–11). Retell the story using the sequence strips.

Sarah asks her father not to shoot a deer.

Chapters 1–3

Indian children visit Sarah.

Chapters 4–7

Sarah is delighted to see her mother, brothers, and sisters again.

Chapters 8–11

The Nobles look at the valley where they will build their house.

Chapters 1–3

John Noble returns to Massachusetts, leaving Sarah behind.

Chapters 4–7

Sarah sleeps in the forest.

Chapters 1–3

John Noble adds a shed and a fence to their cave.

Chapters 4–7

Sarah's father returns.

Chapters 8–11

The Nobles spend the night at the Robinsons' home.

Chapters 1–3

Sarah becomes friends with the Indian children.

Chapters 4–7

A wolf's howling scares Sarah.

Chapters 1–3

Sarah prays for her Indian "family."

Chapters 8–11

Tall John's squaw makes moccasins for Sarah.

Chapters 8–11

The Nobles find a cave in which to stay.

Chapters 4–7

Tall John and his family bring Sarah into their home.

Chapters 8–11

Log Cabin Sequencing *(cont.)*

Directions: Make three copies of the cabin for each student. Cut out the cabins. Number the cabins 1–3 in the box. Follow the directions on page 25 to complete the activity.

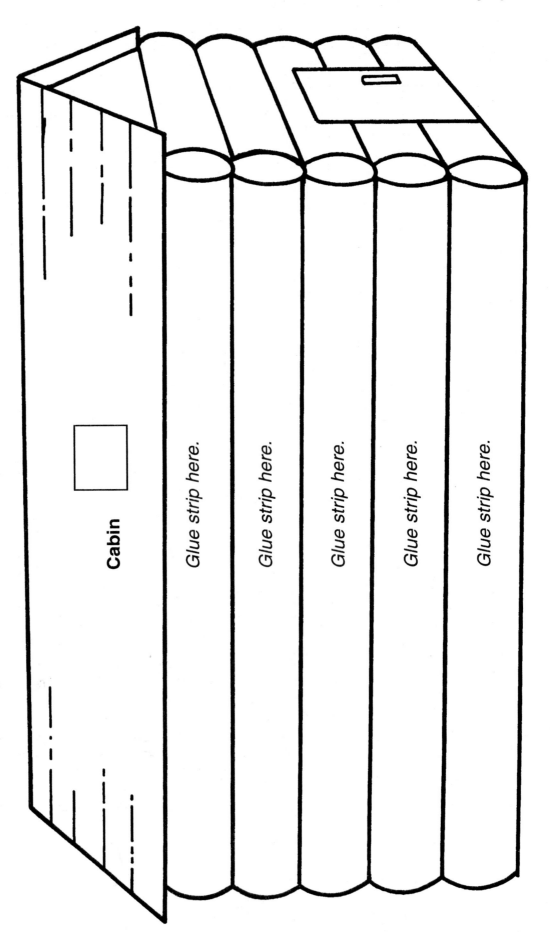

Cabin

Glue strip here.

Glue strip here.

Glue strip here.

Glue strip here.

Glue strip here.

Animal Research Project

Directions: Follow the steps below to complete an animal research project with the students.

1. Review the meaning of warm-blooded animals with the students.

2. The list below shows the nine warm-blooded animals mentioned in *The Courage of Sarah Noble*. Assign an animal to each student. (You will have to assign the same animal to two or three children.)

> ### Animals from *The Courage of Sarah Noble*
>
> | bear | fox | skunk |
> |------|-------|-----------|
> | deer | horse | wolf |
> | duck | owl | woodchuck |

3. Have the students copy the following questions on paper, leaving four to five blank lines after each.

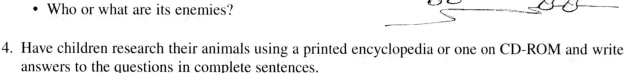

- What type of animal is this (bird or mammal)?

- What does it look like?

- Where does it live?

- How long does it live?

- What does it eat?

- How are its young born?

- Who or what are its enemies?

4. Have children research their animals using a printed encyclopedia or one on CD-ROM and write answers to the questions in complete sentences.

5. Next, have them keyboard their responses (not including the questions) from the paper into the computer, using the available word processing program. Have them save the file and then print out the file so you can check how they are doing.

6. Show them how to put their sentences together into a paragraph. Depending upon your class' needs and abilities, you could do a lesson on combining sentences using conjunctions.

7. If possible, below the paragraph, have the students import a graphic of the animal from a clip art program. Other options include having them use a "draw" program, scan an image, or just draw a picture freehand on the page.

Cloze Paragraph

Directions: Choose the word from the basket below that has the right number of letters to complete each blank. Then read the paragraph and answer the question at the bottom.

WORD BASKET

strawberries	plants	runners	two
ground	root	raspberries	along
more	rose	seeds	

In *The Courage of Sarah Noble,* Sarah picks wild _ _ _ _ _ _ _ _ _ _ _ _ to

add to their evening meals. Strawberries, blackberries, and _ _ _ _ _ _ _ _ _ _ _

are all members of the _ _ _ _ plant family. These kinds of _ _ _ _ _ _ have

_ _ _ ways to reproduce! They grow fruit which falls to the _ _ _ _ _ _ , releases its

_ _ _ _ _ , and starts a new plant. But they also send out _ _ _ _ _ _ _ .

These look like long stems growing _ _ _ _ _ the ground. The runners go down into the

soil and take _ _ _ _ . They start new plants, too. In fact, _ _ _ berry plants begin

from runners than from seeds!

What is so special about berry plants?

_____

_____

_____

Supplies from the General Store

These are the supplies Father bought before the journey to Connecticut.

GENERAL SUPPLIES

cooking pot	$2.00	beans	50¢ a pound	cornmeal	10¢ a pound
hammer	$3.00	corn seeds	25¢ a pound	sugar	10¢ a pound
saw	$5.00	wheat seeds	5¢ a pound	flour	5¢ a pound
axe	$4.75	vegetable seeds	15¢ a pound		

Directions: Solve the problems below. The general store in Massachusetts charged the following prices.

1. The price of a cooking pot was $2.00. John Noble got two, so he paid _____.

2. The price of a hammer was $3.00. John Noble get one, so he paid _____.

3. Beans were 50 cents a pound. He got 9 pounds, so he paid _____.

4. Corn seeds cost 25 cents a pound. He got 4 pounds, so he paid _____.

5. A saw cost $5.00. John Noble got one saw, so he paid _____.

6. Cornmeal went for 10 cents a pound. He got 6 pounds, so he paid _____.

7. Wheat seeds cost 5 cents a pound. He got 7 pounds, so he paid _____.

8. John Noble bought an axe which cost $4.75, so he paid _____.

9. Vegetable seeds sold for 15 cents a pound. He got 4 pounds, so he paid _____.

10. Sugar sold for 10 cents a pound. He bought 25 pounds, so he paid _____.

11. Flour sold for 5 cents a pound. Mr. Noble got 25 pounds, so he paid _____.

12. What was his total bill at the general store? _____.

Word Problems

Directions: Complete the following word problems. Show all your work and be sure to use a label with each answer.

1. John Noble had to cut down 15 trees to complete one wall of his cabin. He had to cut down an additional 5 trees for each side of his roof. How many trees did he cut down to construct the whole cabin? _____

2. The Nobles brought 9 pounds of dried beans with them. If they used ½ pound of beans to make enough bean porridge for one dinner, how many dinners could they eat before they ran out of beans? _____

3. John Noble worked 9 hours each day when building his cabin. It took him 95 days to complete his work. How many total hours of his labor did it take to complete the cabin?

   _____

4. Tall John helped John Noble build his cabin. He worked for Mr. Noble for 3 hours each day for 62 days. How many total hours did he work? _____

5. Using the answers you got in #3 and #4, how many total hours did it take for both men to build the Noble home? _____

6. Sarah stayed with Tall John and his family for 6 weeks and 2 days. How many total days did she live with them? _____

7. It was a journey of 349 miles for Sarah and her father to travel from their home in Massachusetts to where they would have a new home in New Milford. On his way to get the rest of the family, some friendly Indians told John Noble about a shortcut that would save him 22 miles, so he followed it. How many miles did John Noble travel on his return trip to Massachusetts? _____

8. How many miles ROUND TRIP did John Noble travel when he went to get the rest of his family and brought them to the new home? (Remember he took the shortcut both ways.)

   _____

Directed Manipulatives and Center Activities

Before doing this activity, ask the students to clear their desktops so they can focus on the lesson. Then, using the pattern pieces you made for the children to design Sarah's quilt (page 40), give each child two of the large triangles, four of the small triangles, and one of the squares.

1. Have everyone hold up one large right triangle. Explain that this is a right triangle because it has a corner like a rectangle's corner.

2. Have everyone hold up one small right triangle. Explain that this is an isosceles right triangle because it has two equal sides. (They might notice that the large triangle is an isosceles, too.)

3. Have everyone hold up his or her square. Explain that it is a special rectangle because all four of its sides are the same length.

4. Ask the students to take their two large triangles and form a square. Circulate around the room to ensure everyone is successful.

5. Have the students put two small triangles together to form a larger right triangle. Ask them if it is equal to any other pieces they have. They should respond, "Yes, to the large triangles." Tell them these are called equivalent triangles.

6. Ask them to put the four small triangles together to form a familiar shape. Ask what shape they created. They should respond, "square."

7. On the chalkboard or overhead projector, use pieces similar to theirs to create a trapezoid, and ask them to create it on their desktops. Make a trapezoid with the four small triangles. Circulate around the room to ensure everyone is successful. Ask if anyone knows the name of the shape. Ask what makes it different from a rectangle. (*the sloping sides and lack of right angles*)

8. Depending on your children's abilities, you can model this for them or ask them to create it themselves. Have them combine four small triangles and one large triangle to create a five-sided polygon. Ask if anyone knows what this is called. (*a pentagon*)

9. On the chalkboard or overhead projector, draw a hexagon. Challenge the students to make the same shape with their pieces. Circulate around the room to ensure everyone is successful. Ask if anyone knows the name of the shape. (*a hexagon*) Ask how many sides it has. (*six sides*)

Extension Ideas

- When you have completed this guided lesson, collect all the pattern pieces and set up a center. Rotate children through it, having them create geometric shapes. Have each student trace the outlines of the shapes created on paper and then color them. Display these designs on a bulletin board or wall in the room.

- Provide additional copies of the nine-patch quilt block on page 40 and let the students use the template pieces to create additional designs to color and display. You can also display the traditional quilt block patterns shown at the top of page 41.

Western Connecticut Map

Directions: The roads and highways of today are often based on the trails used by the Indians and settlers hundreds of years ago. Using the map on page 33, answer the following questions.

1. Find and circle New Milford.

2. Use a yellow crayon or marker to trace a probable route the Nobles took from Massachusetts to Connecticut.

3. What is the modern name for the Great River near which they lived? _____

4. What lake is near New Milford? _____ Color it blue.

5. The town of New Milford, Connecticut, is near the border of what state? _____ Trace the border with a red crayon or marker.

6. Use a ruler to draw a straight line connecting Milford with New Milford. Then, using the scale provided, figure out the distance between the two places. _____

7. How far is New Milford from the nearest state border?

   _____

8. If you made a living by catching fish, in what town would you most likely settle? _____

9. What is the name of the state that is north of New Milford?_____ Color its border with a brown crayon or marker.

10. What is the name of the very large body of water that is south of New Milford and runs along Connecticut's coast?

    _____

Western Connecticut Map *(cont.)*

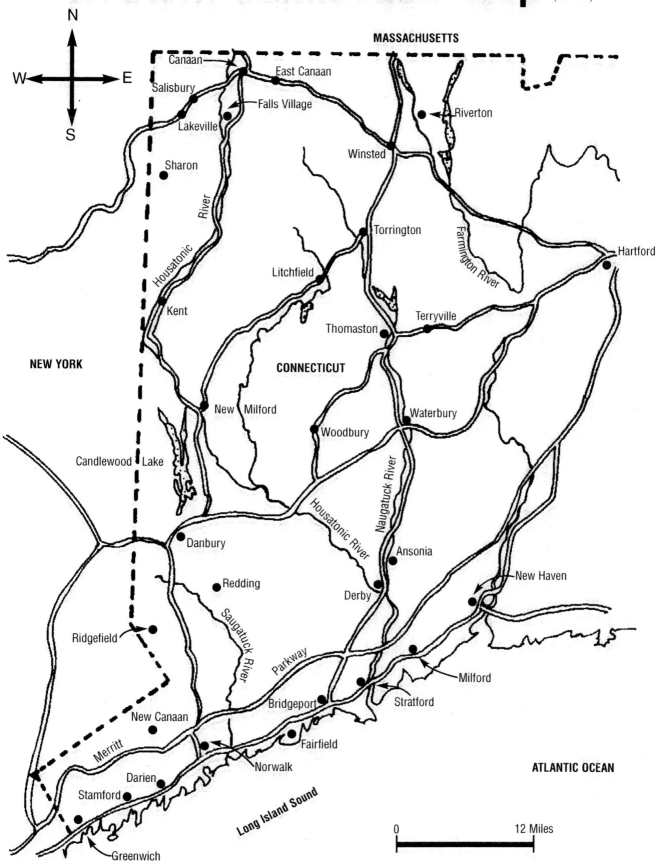

MASSACHUSETTS

N
W E
S

Canaan
East Canaan
Salisbury
Falls Village
Lakeville
Riverton
Sharon
Winsted

Housatonic River

Torrington
Farmington River
Hartford

Litchfield

Kent
Terryville
Thomaston

CONNECTICUT

NEW YORK

New Milford
Waterbury
Woodbury

Candlewood Lake

Housatonic River
Naugatuck River

Danbury
Ansonia

Redding
New Haven
Derby

Ridgefield
Saugatuck River

Parkway
Milford
Bridgeport
Stratford

New Canaan
Fairfield

Merritt
Norwalk
ATLANTIC OCEAN

Darien
Stamford

Long Island Sound

Greenwich

0   12 Miles

Food Processing Techniques of the 1700s

Objective: To understand how difficult it was to grow and store food in the "good old days."

Overview of activity: Photocopy and distribute page 36 to the students. Instruct them to use crayons or markers ONLY when you say to do so. You will read the script below, stopping at the indicated points to have the children color one of the picture frames. Then you will read from the script again, stop, and have the children color. This process will repeat until you have completed all eight frames. Or, if it better meets the needs of your students, have them do the first four frames one day and, using the same procedure, complete the final four frames the next day. As an extension, have the children make bean porridge from dried beans, using the recipe given on page 35.

TEACHER'S SCRIPT

"In the 1700s, growing, storing, and preparing enough food to eat occupied almost every waking hour of a person's day. You could not go to a grocery store or a restaurant to buy food, so almost everyone grew his own. The vegetables grown had to be eaten within 10 days, or they would start to spoil."

STOP: Have children color their first frame—a picture of someone working in a field of beans. Allow about 60–90 seconds.

"At a general store, you could buy staples, which were the basic foods everyone used, such as flour, sugar, cornmeal, and dried vegetables. Refrigerators, freezers, and packaging had not been invented yet, so the only way to keep vegetables from spoiling over an extended period of time was to dry them. Unfortunately, some of the food's vitamins were lost during this long and involved process."

STOP: Have the children color the second frame on their page—the interior of a general store. Allow about 90 seconds for this.

"In the story, Sarah served her father bean porridge made from dried beans. They may have dried the beans themselves or purchased them already dried at a general store. Either way, the drying process was the same. To discourage spoilage from the molds, bacteria, and yeast present in all foods, almost every bit of moisture had to be removed from the beans. First, the beans were steam blanched to kill germs in them. This was done by dipping the beans into boiling water and holding them there for half a minute."

STOP: Have the children color the third frame on their page—the steam blanching of the beans. Allow about 60–90 seconds for this.

"Then the beans were handpicked to select the best ones, since imperfect beans might eventually spoil the good ones and ruin the whole lot. Next, the beans were spread out on cloth-lined trays to dry in the sun. Unfortunately, most climates do not have enough sun, so this was supplemented by heating them in an oven. The heat had to begin at about 120° F (49° C) and never go higher than 140° F (60° C), which was pretty difficult when using a wood-fired stove. The best drying racks were made to move back and forth from sun heat to oven heat, as the weather allowed. Every single hour the beans on the trays had to be individually turned by hand to allow even drying on all sides. If the humidity was low and the days very sunny, two days might be enough to completely dry the beans. Each day before sundown, all food drying outdoors had to be brought inside to protect it from the dew that settled at night."

STOP: Have the children color the fourth frame on the page—the drying box. Allow about 60 seconds for this.

Food Processing Techniques of the 1700s *(cont.)*

TEACHER'S SCRIPT *(cont.)*

"After the beans had cooled from the day's heat, they were stirred on their trays. When the beans were brittle and tough and rattled on the tray, they were ready to be conditioned."

STOP: Have the children color the fifth frame on their page—stirring the beans on their trays. Allow about 60 seconds for this.

"To condition the beans, the person placed them in an enamel or graniteware crock, covered it with a cloth, and placed it in a warm, airy room for 10 to 14 days. During this time, the beans had to be stirred twice a day and any pieces that seemed limp or moist were removed."

STOP: Have the children color the sixth frame on their page—a crock covered with a cloth. Allow about 60 seconds for this.

"At the end of the conditioning time, the remaining beans were loosely arranged on trays and placed in an oven of about 175° F (79° C) for about 15 minutes to kill any remaining bacteria. After the beans were removed from the oven and had cooled, they were placed into cloth bags."

STOP: Have the children color the seventh frame on their page—the beans sliding off the trays into cloth bags. Allow about 60–90 seconds.

"After the drying process, the beans would be edible for at least four months. Before they could be eaten, they needed reconstitution. Sarah reconstituted them by adding just enough cold water to cover them and then soaking them all day until they swelled up to their original size. Then she heated them slowly over the campfire."

STOP: Have the children color the eighth frame on their page—Sarah stirring a pot of beans over a campfire. Allow about 90 seconds.

Extension: Have the children make bean porridge from dried beans, using this recipe:

1. Purchase a one-pound bag (450 g) of dried navy beans. White beans originated in America and were introduced to the settlers by the Indians. The "navy" name came about because these beans earned a reputation for keeping well on long sea voyages.

2. Early in the morning of the day you plan to serve the porridge, put 1 to 2 cups (240 to 480 mL) in a pot with an equal amount of water to soak. The beans will swell to twice their size, so 2 cups (480 mL) will yield 4 cups (960 mL). Navy beans are the toughest kind and thus require the longest soaking time. Remove any beans that float, as this can be a sign that that particular bean has bacteria inside it. Explain to the children why you are removing the floaters and that Sarah would have done the same thing.

3. Gradually heat the beans to boiling, and allow them to simmer for five minutes. (**Note:** If you forget to soak, bring the beans to a boil and simmer for 3 minutes, then leave tightly covered for one hour before serving.)

4. Once the beans are soft, mix in 2 tablespoons (30 mL) of flour. Add salt and pepper to taste and then cook for another three minutes.

5. Serve the porridge in tiny paper cups. Since the porridge will seem incredibly tasteless and unappealing to children who eat modern American fare, your students probably will not want much more than a taste of it.

Food Processing Techniques of the 1700s *(cont.)*

Directions: Color each picture ONLY when your teacher tells you to do so.

Making a Wigwam

Sarah lived in Tall John's wigwam. There are three stages to the construction of a wigwam.

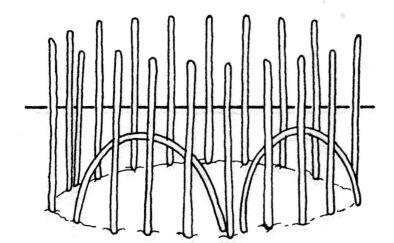

Stage 1

Sixteen to twenty long poles were planted in the ground about 15 feet (4.6 m) across.

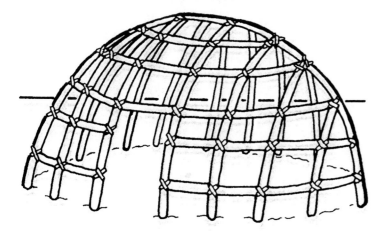

Stage 2

These poles were bent and lashed together with strips of bark. Two or three rings of saplings were tied around the structure to give it strength. The domed shape kept the heat close to the ground.

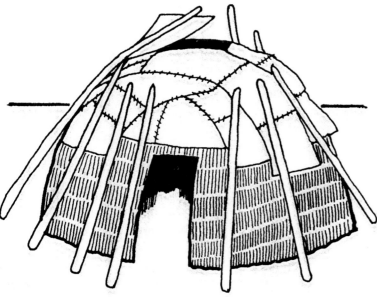

Stage 3

To cover the outside, the Indians used birch or elm bark, animal hides, or even mats of cattails sewn together. In cold weather, all three would be used to insulate the home.

A hole was left in the top of the wigwam to allow smoke to escape from the fire built on the floor in the center. The rest of the floor was covered with fir branches topped with animal skins to create a warm carpet.

Games Sarah Played with the Indian Children

As soon as they could walk, little boys used toy bows and arrows to shoot at a target set up on a log. Older boys used their toy bows and arrows to shoot at a rolling hoop, since a hunter often needed to shoot moving prey. Girls had dolls without faces, as they feared that the tiny people (like elves) who lived in the woods might grow angry if dolls looked too much like them. These dolls were usually made of cornhusks or corncobs, although some have been found that were made of bark or wood. Both boys and girls played the games explained here.

Dice

Materials (for each group of three students): paper and pencil for scores, two smooth, flat stones or peach pits painted blue on one side and red on the other or with a different number of lines on each side (Smooth, flat stones were collected and painted a different color or with a different number of lines or dots on each face to create a die. If flat stones could not be found, fruit pits, bones, wood, or beaver teeth were used.)

Directions: Play this in front of the class with a volunteer to establish the scoring routine, and then put the children into groups of three. Assign a scorekeeper for each group. Have each group take their dice and take turns tossing them inside a small basket or margarine bowl. One child takes red, the other takes blue, and the third takes mixed. When two red dice come up, the red child scores two points; if two blue come up, the blue child scores two points; and when one of each comes up, the mixed child scores two points. One round consists of 10 throws. If scored correctly, the three scores added together will equal 20. It is a fair game, so if you play it enough, everyone should have a chance to win (statistically, anyway).

    Sample game: Group consists of Ben (red), Rachel (blue), and Amanda (mixed)

           1st throw: Two red dice up—Ben scores 2 points
           2nd throw: Two red dice up—Ben scores 2 points
           3rd throw: Both blue dice up—Rachel scores 2 points
           4th throw: One red up, one blue up—Amanda scores 2 points
           5th throw: One red up, one blue up—Amanda scores 2 points
           6th throw: One red up, one blue up—Amanda scores 2 points
           7th throw: Two red dice up—Ben scores 2 points
           8th throw: Both blue dice up—Rachel scores 2 points
           9th throw: Both red dice up—Ben scores 2 points
           10th throw: Two red dice up—Ben scores 2 points
           Ending score: Ben = 10 points, Rachel = 4 points, Amanda = 6 points

Guessing Game

Materials: pebbles for one-third of the class

Directions: This traditional Indian game was the one that Sarah played with the children in the book. Put the students in groups of three, and have two volunteers in each group take off their shoes. If someone is wearing sandals, that person cannot be a volunteer. Two of the children turn around. The other child takes a pebble and hides it under one of four shoes. Then the children turn around, and each one tries to guess where the pebble is. The children rotate the task of hiding the pebble and guessing. There is no scoring in this game.

Games Sarah Played
with the Indian Children *(cont.)*

Cat's Cradle

Materials: lengths of string about 24" (61 cm) long for half the class (For string, the Indians used pine tree roots or the inner lining of bark woven into a rope.)

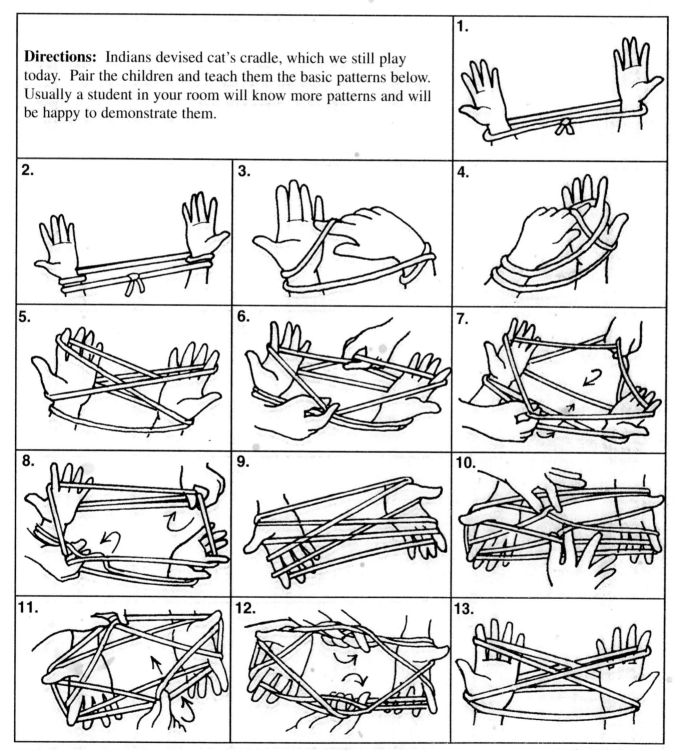

Directions: Indians devised cat's cradle, which we still play today. Pair the children and teach them the basic patterns below. Usually a student in your room will know more patterns and will be happy to demonstrate them.

Quilt Pieces

Directions for Teacher

1. Make a set of quilt pieces for each child in your class by photocopying this page onto oaktag. Each child should get four small triangles, two large triangles, and one square. After the pieces are cut, laminate them for greater durability and reuse.

2. Have the children design their own nine-patch quilt block with page 41.

3. When the children have completed their quilt blocks, glue them all together on a large piece of butcher paper and display the class quilt in the classroom or hallway under the banner: Sarah Noble's Quilt, circa 1707.

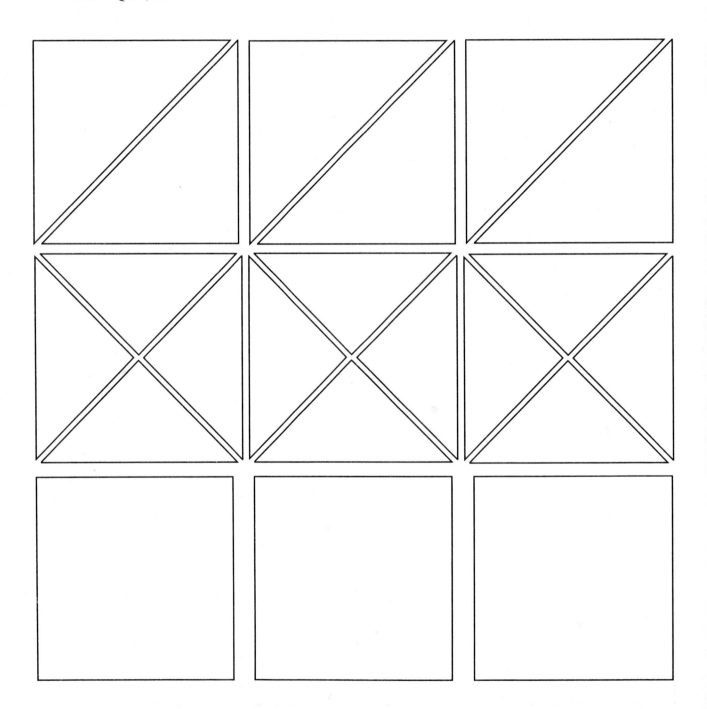

Designing Sarah's Quilt

Directions: Think of what Sarah's quilt looks like when you read about her lying on it in the forest, on Mistress Robinson's floor, or in the cave. Use the pattern pieces to show a quilt block from Sarah's quilt. Trace around the pieces to draw lines in the right places. You may copy one of the designs below or create your own. Name and color your design.

Tree Everlasting   **Friendship Star**   **Ohio Star**   **Pinwheel**   **Letter X**

Games Indian Children Played

The Indian children played games for several reasons. One reason was to make life more fun. The games also helped to develop strong bodies that would be capable of adult tasks. Another reason was to learn how to follow rules, share, and take turns. The games also taught the children survival skills.

Indians used balls made of inflated animal bladders covered with deerskin. Team sports were often played with teams of both boys and girls, although there were exceptions.

Directions: Arrange with the physical education teacher to have the children play some games that originated with Indians, including some of the team sports we play today, such as tug-of-war, wrestling, lacrosse, field hockey, and bowling. In addition to these familiar games, the physical education teacher might want to try some of the games below.

Kick Ball Relay

Place the children in teams of four. Give each team a ball. The object is to kick the ball down the length of the gym or field to a predetermined line and then all the way back. The next player in the team has to do the same. The first team of runners to kick the ball all the way to the line and back wins.

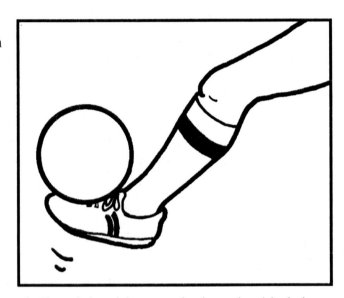

This was actually a game played by the Plains Indians who set a goal miles away. All the team members began kicking a rock at the same time, and the team that had all the runners finish won.

Mixed-Up Soccer Football

Boys play against girls. Boys can only kick the soccer ball, and the girls can only throw it with their hands. To score, a team must take or get the ball (by either kicking or throwing) through two goal posts set up at the ends of a long field.

The Mahicans played this game throughout the summer because they believed it helped their crops to grow.

Top Game

Children sit in circles of four around a top. The first child starts the top spinning, then jumps up and runs all the way around the gym once. If he or she does not make it back before the top stops spinning, he or she is out of the game. Play continues in this fashion until all but one child is eliminated. That child is declared the winner.

During pioneer times, American Indian children ran out of the wigwam and around the outside once before returning. Based on your students' age and abilities, you may need to establish a different distance to run.

Using the Internet

The Courage of Sarah Noble was written about 50 years ago, but it is still in print today because children have enjoyed it so much.

Directions

1. Put the following sentence starters on the board or overhead:

   I liked (disliked) this book because_____.

   I would (not) recommend this book to a friend because _____.

2. Explain to the children that they need to complete each sentence in a short and simple but specific way. You may want to give them examples (see below).

   I like this book because I felt like I got to know Sarah.

   I would recommend this book to a friend because I liked the ending.

   I disliked this book because I thought that Sarah's father should never have left her with the Indians.

   I would not recommend this book to a friend because I didn't think it was exciting enough.

3. Look at their answers prior to letting them go to the computer. "It's neat" and "It was fun" are unacceptable responses (if your children are capable of more). Tell them their answers must include something about the story.

4. Have the children take their papers with their answers on them to the computer.

5. Ask your students to go to this Web site: *http://www.amazon.com*

6. Help the children navigate to the book *The Courage of Sarah Noble,* choose the "write a review" option, and type in their prepared comments from their papers.

Stick Puppet Theater

Make a puppet theater for the children to use in the classroom. The patterns and directions for making the stick puppets are on page 45.

Materials

- large empty cardboard box (Appliance boxes are especially good.)
- markers, crayons, or paints and paintbrushes
- scissors or a craft knife (knife for adult use only)
- strips of Velcro® (optional)

Directions

1. Determine which side will be the front, and cut out the top, bottom, and back of the box.
2. Using the existing folds of the box, bend the sides so they flare out to provide the puppeteers with elbow room. See the illustration below.
3. Cut out a window in the front of the box in one of two ways: leaving the "shutters" on so you can close the curtain by shutting them, or cutting out a large window area and draping a cloth behind it, which the children move while performing. If you leave the shutters on, you will need to use Velcro on the back sides of the shutters and the front of the theater to keep the shutters from closing during the performances.
4. Have the children decorate the outside of the theater with scenes and people from the book: the forest, the Great River, wigwams, Sarah and her father, the log cabin, the cave, the fence, Tall John and his children, Thomas the horse, etc.

Using the Puppets and Theater

1. Make stick puppets, using the patterns and directions on page 45. (They may be enlarged if you wish.) Laminate them for greater durability.
2. Write a script with your class, outlining the most important events in the story.
3. Have small groups of students take turns reading the parts and using the stick puppets while the rest of the class serves as an audience. They may also enjoy performing for another teacher's class, school administrators, or parents.
4. Have the students create a new adventure for Sarah Noble, using the puppets and theater to tell their stories. If additional characters are needed, the students can make their own puppets.

Stick Puppet Theater *(cont.)*

Directions: Reproduce these patterns onto sturdy tagboard. Cut them along the dashed lines. Have students color them. To complete the stick puppets, glue each pattern to a craft stick. Use the stick puppets with the puppet theater on page 44 as part of your culminating experience.

18th Century Dioramas

Directions

1. Organize the children into groups of three.

2. Have each group build a diorama of one of the following: Tall John's wigwam or the Nobles' log cabin.

3. The following are some ideas to help the children accomplish their task:

   • Obtain a large, flat board or piece of sturdy cardboard which can be made by cutting up big boxes. Just one side of a refrigerator box can provide two large platforms.

   • Cover the board by gluing moss, grass, or crumbled dead leaves to the surface. Materials will vary based on availability. Poster paints can also be used to paint the board. Depending on the season the group chooses, boards can be covered with cotton.

   • Use small margarine tubs covered with tree bark (for the wigwams) or small boxes covered with craft sticks (for the logs in the cabin). Be sure to help the children cut any necessary doors, windows, or other openings.

   • Construct the chimney on the Noble home with pieces of cardboard glued to the main house and anchored to the board with both glue and clay. Make certain the children decorate (color) it prior to attaching it to the diorama. If they want to make a genuine fieldstone chimney, have them press tiny pebbles into modeling clay and attach it to the house and board.

   • Use modeling clay to create figures (people and animals) and to anchor things to the board.

   • Use sticks for trees. Sticks from fir trees with the needles cut short make good pine trees.

   • Depending on the season the group chooses, the trees can be "leafed out" with glued-on tiny bits of green, yellow, or orange yarn or covered with cotton.

   • Special touches should be encouraged—a campfire made of small sticks glued in a triangular fashion, stack of "logs" glued near the outside of the cabin or wigwam, a fence outlining a paddock area for Thomas and constructed of craft sticks or twigs glued together and fastened to the board with clay.

Bibliography

Other Books by Alice Dalgliesh

The Bears on Hemlock Mountain. Aladdin Paperbacks, 1991.

> (Grades K–3) A suspenseful tale of an 8-year-old boy who must cross Hemlock Mountain but is afraid of encountering a bear. A Newbery Honor book.

El Corage De Sarah Noble. Noguery Caralt Editores, 1997.

> (Grades K–3) Spanish language edition of *The Courage of Sarah Noble.*

The Fourth of July Story. Aladdin Paperbacks, 1995.

> (Grades K–3) A simple, clearly written introduction to the events and people who helped bring about America's independence from British rule.

The Silver Pencil. Puffin Paperbacks, 1991.

> (Grades 3–6) Touching historical fiction detailing a young woman's growing writing talent as she copes with moving from Scotland to England and finally to America. A Newbery Honor book. Since it is written for young adults, you'd probably need to read this aloud to your class.

Thanksgiving Story. Aladdin Paperbacks, 1985.

> (Grades K–3) The engaging story of a Pilgrim family's struggle for survival in the harsh New World which culminates in a Thanksgiving feast with their new Indian friends.

Little House Series by Laura Ingalls Wilder

This series tells the story of Laura Ingalls Wilder's life, beginning with her 1867 birth in a tiny log cabin in the wild Big Woods of Wisconsin. The books tell how Laura and her pioneer family travel and settle first in Kansas, then in Minnesota, and finally the Dakota Territory.

Little House in the Big Woods. HarperTrophy, 1971.

Little House on the Prairie. HarperTrophy, 1973.

On the Banks of Plum Creek. HarperTrophy, 1973.

By the Shores of Silver Lake. HarperTrophy, 1973.

The Long Winter. HarperTrophy, 1971.

Little Town on the Prairie. HarperTrophy, 1973.

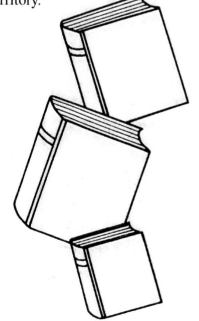

Answer Key

Page 24

Pages 25–26

Cabin 1: Chapters 1–3

1. Sarah sleeps in the forest.
2. A wolf's howling scares Sarah.
3. The Nobles spend the night at the Robinsons' home.
4. Sarah asks her father not to shoot a deer.
5. The Nobles look at the valley where they will build their house.

Cabin 2: Chapters 4–7

6. The Nobles find a cave in which to stay.
7. John Noble adds a shed and a fence to their cave.
8. Indian children visit Sarah.
9. Sarah becomes friends with the Indian children.
10. John Noble returns to Massachusetts, leaving Sarah behind.

Cabin 3: Chapters 8–11

11. Tall John and his family bring Sarah into their home.
12. Sarah prays for her Indian "family."
13. Tall John's squaw makes moccasins for Sarah.
14. Sarah's father returns.

15. Sarah is delighted to see her mother, brothers, and sisters again.

Page 28

strawberries, raspberries, rose, plants, two, ground, seeds, runners, along, root, more

Berry plants are special because they have two ways to reproduce. One way is from seeds, and the other is from runners.

Page 29

1. $4.00
2. $3.00
3. $4.50
4. $1.00
5. $5.00
6. $0.60
7. $0.35
8. $4.75
9. $0.60
10. $2.50
11. $1.25
12. $27.55

Page 30

1. 70 trees
2. 18 dinners
3. 855 hours
4. 186 hours
5. 1,041 hours
6. 44 days
7. 327 miles
8. 654 miles

Page 32

3. Housatonic River
4. Candlewood Lake
5. New York
6. 28 miles or 45 km (3½" or 9 cm)
7. 6 miles or 10 km (¾" or 2 cm)
8. Fairfield
9. Massachusetts
10. Long Island Sound or Atlantic Ocean